Happy Coloring!

Heather Land

HEATHER'S ADULT COLORING BOOKS
www.HeatherLandBooks.com

THIS BOOK IS DEDICATED

TO THOSE WE LOVE

AND THOSE WE'VE LOST

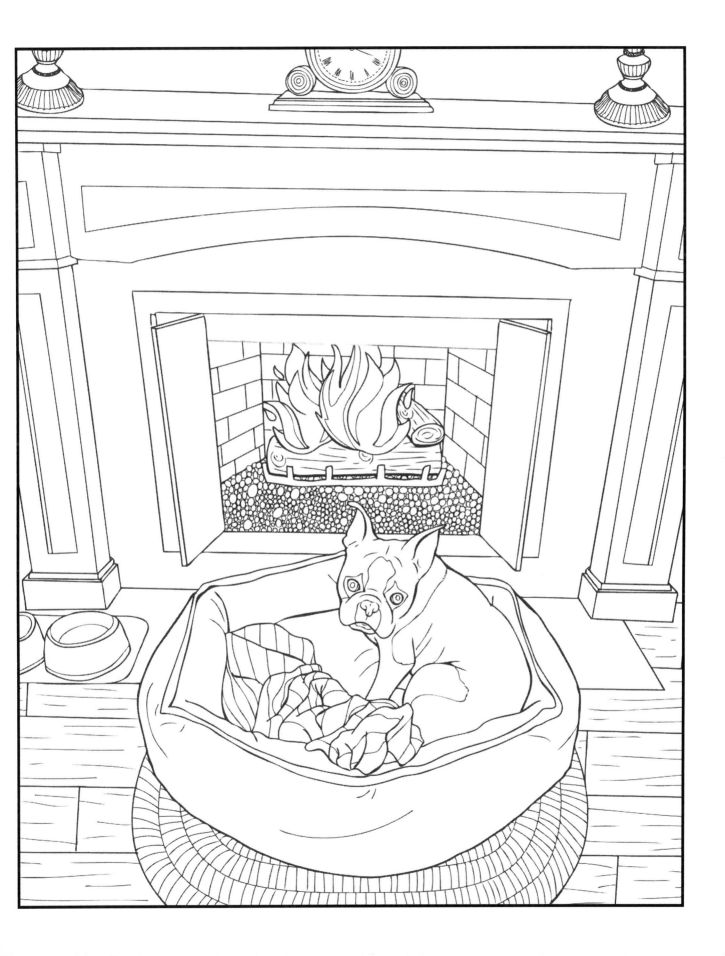

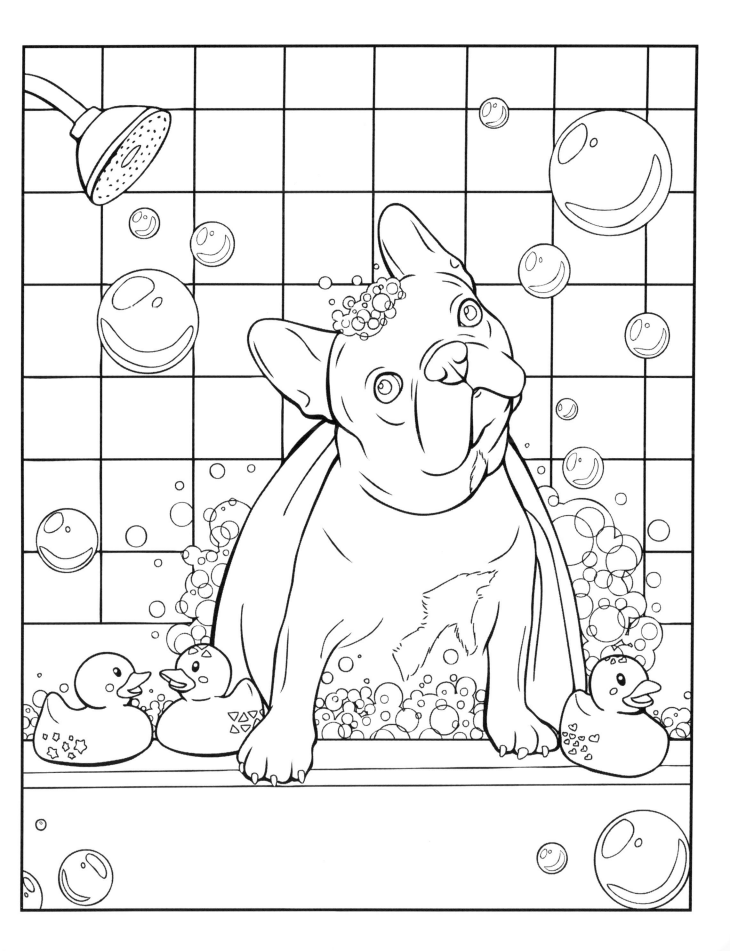

COLOR TEST SQUARES

TEST YOUR COLORS HERE AND USE THIS
PAGE AS A REFERENCE GUIDE

Pinterest.

COLOR TEST SQUARES

TEST YOUR COLORS HERE AND USE THIS
PAGE AS A REFERENCE GUIDE

Pinterest.

Thank you to the following people for allowing your Frenchies to be featured in this book. Without you, this book would not exist!

Taylor Wilson
Aimée Mcluckie
Lauren Fisher Stofle
JC Jison
Diana Ray Miller
Denise Bertino
Kari S Ryan
Kristie Matthews
Ally Lauren
Georgette Artis
Emily Carlson
Colleen Curley
Desiree Montoya
Sylvia Kroon
Amy E Denoncourt
Mackenzie Ann
Shaun Taylor DuVall
Chuck Lombardo
Doria Bybee
Cherie Lee Heid
Mandy Omiecinski
Cheri Jensen
Tracey Ales Rymer
Rebekah Logie
Elishia Dixon
Kaitlain Amblo

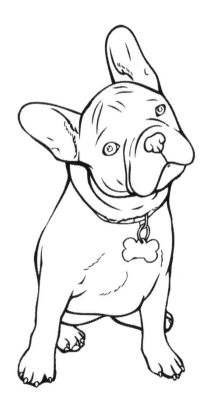

Made in the USA
Middletown, DE
16 October 2022

12861594R00040